EGMONT
We bring stories to life

First published in Great Britain in 2020 by Egmont UK Limited
2 Minster Court, 10th Floor, London EC3R 7BB

Written by Stephanie Milton
Edited by Craig Jelley
Designed by John Stuckey, Andrea Philpots and Ian Pollard
Illustrations by Ryan Marsh
Production by Louis Harvey and Laura Grundy
Special thanks to Alex Wiltshire, Jennifer Hammervald, Filip Thoms,
Amanda Ström, Kelsey Howard and Nathan Rose.

ISBN 978 1 4052 9834 6

71038/001
Printed in Italy

ONLINE SAFETY FOR YOUNGER FANS

Spending time online is great fun! Here are a few simple rules to help younger fans stay safe
and keep the internet a great place to spend time:

- Never give out your real name – don't use it as your username.
- Never give out any of your personal details.
- Never tell anybody which school you go to or how old you are.
- Never tell anybody your password except a parent or a guardian.
- Be aware that you must be 13 or over to create an account on many sites. Always check
the site policy and ask a parent or guardian for permission before registering.
- Always tell a parent or guardian if something is worrying you.

Stay safe online. Any website addresses listed in this book are correct at the time of going to print.
However, Egmont is not responsible for content hosted by third parties. Please be aware that online
content can be subject to change and websites can contain content that is unsuitable for children.
We advise that all children are supervised when using the internet.

Egmont takes its responsibility to the planet and its inhabitants very seriously.
We aim to use papers from well-managed forests run by responsible suppliers.

GUIDE TO MINECRAFT DUNGEONS

MOJANG

A HANDBOOK FOR HEROES

CONTENTS

ADVENTURE AWAITS

Dungeons is an entirely new game set in Minecraft's endless worlds. You'll see the realm from a new perspective as you hack and slash your way through new foes in a quest to rid the world of the Arch-Illager. Read on to discover all you need to know about Dungeons and save the world from certain doom!

THE TRAGEDY OF THE ARCH-ILLAGER

IT WAS A TIME OF GREAT ADVENTURE ... AND DANGER.

Shunned by his kin, an Illager wandered the land, seeking a new home. But all he found was hatred. Driven by rage against those who wronged him, he wandered blind to whatever end. Until at long last, the Illager found something that would change him forever ...

THE ORB OF DOMINANCE.

Corrupted by evil, driven by vengeance, the Arch-Illager made all bow before him. If they did not bow, they would fall and so the Illagers raided the land.

Who would have the valour, the purity of heart, to stand against the Arch-Illager's reign of terror?

MAYBE ... YOU?

DUNGEONS PRIMER

Dungeons is perfect for any Minecraft fan looking for a brand new challenge. It might look fairly familiar, but it plays completely differently to what you'd expect. For the uninitiated, here's a quick guide to get you up to speed on this epic new blockbuster.

SWORD PLAY

The core gameplay of Dungeons is defeating enemies with a variety of different weapons – sometimes this kind of action is known as 'hack and slash'. You'll make your way through levels, cleaving through hordes of enemies, which is as simple as aiming and pressing the attack button.

A REWARDING TASK

When enemies are defeated, they'll drop Emeralds, Experience Points and sometimes a piece of equipment. You can equip a weapon, a bow, armor and three Artifacts at any one time, and you'll want to check to see if any new drops are more powerful than your current equipment.

ENEMIES

The mobs of the world come in all shapes and sizes, and unfortunately, they're all out to get you. As you progress through the game, you'll fight bigger and badder enemies, but get greater rewards for doing so. Just make sure you keep equipping stronger weapons and you'll have no problem advancing.

THE GAME SCREEN

1. STATUS ICON
This tells you any statuses that are currently applied to you, good or bad.

2. INVENTORY
Where all your loot is stored. You can change your equipped items, including Artifacts.

3. HOT KEYS
These show your equipped Artifacts, potions, map and dodge timer, as well as the button binding for each one.

4. HEART
Tracks your current health – if it's almost empty, chug a potion to top it back up again.

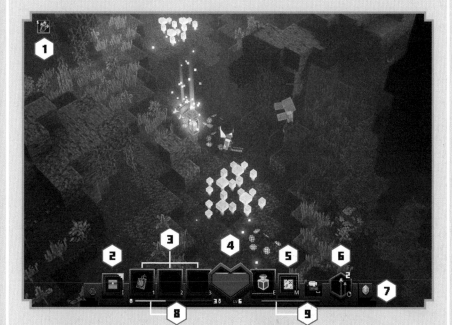

5. MAP
This will take you to the map screen, where you can see how much of the map you've discovered and your current objectives.

6. QUIVER
Tells you how many arrows you have left to loose on the wandering mob masses.

7. EMERALDS
The currency of the world. The more of these you have, the more equipment you can buy!

8. SOULS
Counts how many defeated souls you've managed to collect. These can be used to charge powerful Artifacts.

9. LEVEL AND EXPERIENCE
Tracks how close you are to reaching the next level and unlocking upgrades or rewards.

A TIME FOR HEROES

By the Arch-Illager's decree, we Villagers are now enemies of the Illager empire. As their forces emerge from the dark of forests and caverns and raid our lands, we have but one hope: you. Our fate lies in your hands, brave hero!

CHOOSING YOUR SKIN

Before you begin your quest, you will need to choose a skin fit for a hero. There are many different options for you to choose. The four heroes you see on this page are among the bravest in the land, and it is their journey that we will follow in this book.

YOUR QUEST

You must fight your way through every level until you defeat the Arch-Illager. There are three difficulties for you to attempt. Completing all nine levels in normal mode will unlock Adventure mode – a greater difficulty in which you will face even more challenging mobs!

You will occasionally see these boxes throughout this book with tips and secrets from the Dungeons development team – these can help you survive Dungeons.

LOOT DROPS

More dangerous modes like the Adventure setting will give you better loot, and completing it will unlock Apocalypse difficulty. Only the truest warriors can hope to complete Apocalypse, but the amount of valuable loot you'll find will more than make up for it.

A HERO'S INVENTORY

You cannot hope to succeed in your quest without equipping the powerful gear you'll find as you progress. Familiarise yourself with your inventory, where you'll choose which armor, weapons, Artifacts and enchantments you'll wield in battle.

ENCHANTMENT POINTS

Enchantments power up your gear with special effects. You buy them with Enchantment Points, which are another form of currency. You'll earn an Enchantment Point each time you level-up. Look for this purple icon on your screen to see how many you have.

INVENTORY TABS

Your items are sorted into tabs for easy viewing. You can search through any category individually – like melee, ranged, armor and Artifacts – or scroll through everything you own in the 'All' tab. Beware: you have limited inventory slots!

EMERALDS

You can use Emeralds as currency in your camp's trading area to purchase items (find out more on pages 26-27). Emeralds are earned by defeating mobs and can also be found in chests. Look out for the Emerald icon to see how many you have!

EQUIPMENT SLOTS

Use these slots to equip your best melee weapon, ranged weapon and armor. These items can be picked up during battle or purchased from the trading area.

POWER

The number you see here is the sum total of the Power of the six items in your equipment and Artifact slots. As your total power increases you'll be able to play through each location on higher difficulty levels, gaining access to better loot.

LEVEL
61

POWER
0

LEVEL

The number next to your character is your current level. Your level bar fills up as you defeat mobs, and once it's full you will be rewarded with a valuable Enchantment Point.

ARTIFACT SLOTS

Artifacts are powerful magic items that utilise souls collected from defeated monsters to provide buffs or cause damage. Use these slots to equip your three favourite Artifacts.

ARMOR

As you battle your way to the Arch-Illager's fortress you'll discover many sets of armor. Each set offers different protections and abilities, and can be customised with enchantments. Try out each new set to see what it can do, as it will lend you special abilities and open up new combat styles. Here are a few of the sets that you might find.

HERO'S ARMOR

A gift bestowed upon only the most lauded heroes, the Hero's Armor reduces damage and has a healing aura that benefits nearby allies. Unfortunately it also attracts the attention of mobs, so its wearer would need to be agile enough to dodge or withstand multiple attacks. An excellent set for the tank of a group.

SPELUNKER ARMOR

This set is modelled after underground explorer garb. It provides the owner with a pet bat, which can be useful to distract enemies while you jump in for some quick attacks.

SOUL ROBE

The ancient and mysterious Soul Robe is said to have been woven with evocation magics and enchantments. Some say that if you stare into its shimmering fabric, you can see souls looking back at you. Not surprisingly, it increases the amount of souls you collect from each enemy.

SPLENDID ROBE

This robe is most often seen draped around followers of the Arch-Illager. It offers a chance to revive on death and increases melee damage, making it suited to those charging into the fray.

MYSTERY ARMOR

Nobody is quite sure what this set is made from, hence it's name. It increases ranged damage and has a small chance to teleport the wearer when they land a hit on an enemy mob. It's perfect for stealthy heroes that like to dart around unpredictably to cause chaos.

FOX ARMOR

This piece strikes fear into the hearts of many foes, as it has a reputation for being quite difficult to pierce. In fact, there's a small chance that enemy attacks will be entirely deflected. Cunning!

FROST BITE

Legend has it that this set of armor can remember the cold winds that flowed under the wings of mountain-dwelling phantoms. The combination of the snow spirit and increased ranged damage means it's a great set for an accurate archer.

WEAPONS

You must arm yourself well if you intend to defeat the waves of dangerous mobs and vanquish the Arch-Illager himself. Luckily, the world is full of lethal weapons in all shapes and sizes that can be used in battle with the Illager hordes. Here are some noteworthy examples that can best aid you in your quest.

SOUL FISTS

These gauntlets are clad with gems containing powerful souls. They deal low damage, but have the 'Relentless Combo' ability, which builds attack power as you land hits. They are ideal for punching Illagers in the face, and have a chance to land some deadly critical hits.

JAILOR'S SCYTHE

This scythe was once belonged to The Jailor of Highblock Keep, a cruel villain. The magical chains it produces have restrained many a Villager over the years – now you can use the same power to bind Illagers in position.

CURSED AXE

Any enemies unfortunate enough to be hit with this wretched axe will be poisoned and take consistent damage. It's best for heroes that like to land a quick blow, dodge away and watch their enemies slowly suffer the poison effects.

FANGS OF FROST

These twin daggers of the northern mountains can turn their victim to solid ice with the slightest of touches, leaving a frozen block behind. It's a good idea to freeze trickier enemies until you've cleared out the weaker of the mobs.

EXPLODING CROSSBOW

This unique crossbow – imbued with the incendiary power of TNT – has a devastating explosive shot, which is great for clearing a passage through a huge horde of mobs.

FERAL SOUL CROSSBOW

Be sure to aim true with this bow if you prefer to avoid ridicule from the whispering souls within. It increases the number of souls you gather and boosts your chance of landing a critical hit.

PURPLE STORM

A small but mighty bow, the Purple Storm packs quite a punch. Each arrow deals just above average damage, but the sheer speed at which it can loose the pointy projectiles means that it's almost without parallel in the bow department.

You're always going to be chasing after even better weapons and gear as you level up - and unique items are always going to bring an extra something to your playstyle.

ENCHANTMENTS

Even the most powerful armor and weapons will benefit from the addition of well-chosen enchantments. Here are just a few of the effects you can add to your items – many of these will mean the difference between life and death.

FRENZIED
ON SOUL ROBE (COMMON)

While you are at less than half health, your attack speed will be increased, so you can take out mobs faster.

CHAINS
ON CUTLASS (COMMON)

Has a good chance to chain a cluster of mobs together and keep them bound for a short time.

RADIANCE
ON SOUL KNIFE
(POWERFUL)

Has a chance of spawning a soothing circular area around yourself, which will heal all allies within the perimeter. It's a great enchantment to consider when you're questing with friends.

CHAIN REACTION

ON LONGBOW
(POWERFUL)

Every arrow that leaves your bow has the chance to spawn five extra arrows on impact, creating a crazy arrow tsunami. It's perfect for dealing with a scattering crowd of mobs.

GROWING
ON SCATTER CROSSBOW (COMMON)

Projectiles fired from your crossbow grow in power as they travel through the air, dealing extra damage to distant targets.

FINAL SHOUT
ON REINFORCED MAIL (POWERFUL)

When health goes below a certain point, all your Artifacts are used automatically, even if they are on cooldown.

You choose your equipment, but also choose how you change it to serve the playstyle you like the most through Enchantments. Spawn fire or shoot multiple arrows - whatever works best for you!

ARTIFACTS

These rare objects are imbued with mysterious powers and are awarded to you each time you complete a level. Artifacts can also be found in black and silver loot chests. They are best used in moments of dire need – when you're swarmed or facing a malevolent boss mob.

CORRUPTED BEACON

The Corrupted Beacon fires an intense magical beam that damages mobs unlucky enough to be in the way. It is capable of causing massive amounts of damage.

Since Artifacts are so powerful, they require a cooldown between uses – a short period of time during which they regain their power and cannot be used.

DEATH CAP MUSHROOM

When consumed, the Death Cap Mushroom sends you into a wild frenzy, allowing you to cleave through your enemies with ease. It increases both your movement speed and attack power.

HARVESTER

This mysterious item siphons the energy of lost souls and redirects that power as an attack of energy to any mobs surrounding you. It's an excellent item to use when you find yourself at low health and with little chance to escape.

LIGHTNING ROD

This magical staff allows the wielder to cause bolts of lightning to strike an area, causing damage and expending souls. It is said to have been crafted by Geomancers in an attempt to harness the power of the sky.

TOTEM OF SHIELDING

When the Totem Of Shielding is used, it emits a circular barrier that will protect you and your fellow warriors from enemy projectiles. It also grants 100 health points.

GONG OF WEAKENING

This ancient gong weakens enemies in a large area around the bearer, decreasing their ability to damage and their defence points. It lasts long enough to wear down most enemies, but has a hefty cooldown between uses.

SOUL HEALER

This amulet heals the most injured ally, whether that is you or a friend. Cold to the touch, it seems to be particularly popular with the Illagers dwelling in woodland mansions. It heals a random amount of health and gathers souls while it works, though it does expend souls whenever it is used.

FRIENDLY FACES

Being a hero can be a great burden, but you do not have to bear it alone. Some of the mobs wandering the land can help you, and there are some that you can call to your aid if you have the right equipment. May your quest be blessed by the appearance of these friendly faces.

PIGGY BANK

This unfortunate creature has somehow acquired a chest full of treasure. Now it is a target for heroes such as yourself, who must hit it repeatedly to retrieve the contents. Naturally, the pig will run away as quickly as its short legs can carry it.

KEY GOLEM

You'll find these cute little mobs hiding throughout the world. You must carry them on your back to a locked door, as they're too afraid to go alone. If you take damage whilst carrying one, it will scurry back to where you found it.

BAT

Bats might be small and weak, but they can be a distraction for enemies. To acquire a bat you'll need to be wearing a set of Spelunker Armor. The bat will flutter after you without question.

LLAMA

If you acquire a Wonderful Wheat Artifact, you will be able to summon a llama. Your new friend will spit at mobs to deal damage. It's disgusting, but effective.

IRON GOLEM

Having an iron golem at your side during battle is a distinct advantage – they can cause great damage with a single swing of their arms and withstand a lot of damage. To summon one, you'll need the Golem Kit Artifact – a rare prize indeed.

WOLF

A hero can summon their very own pet wolf by using a Tasty Bone Artifact. Wolves will attack mobs, but will eventually perish. Fortunately they can be summoned repeatedly – you just have to wait 30 seconds from when your wolf disappears.

HELPFUL ITEMS

Even the mightiest warrior needs a little help from time to time. Fortunately, there are several items that can help a hero gain the upper hand in even the trickiest fray. When you defeat a mob, you may be rewarded with one of the following items.

APPLE

An apple provides a small but immediate health boost.

BREAD

A loaf of bread will restore your health over an extended period.

There are three main things you'll find as you play through a mission: Emeralds, consumables such as food or TNT, and more permanent things like weapons, armor, and Artifacts.

PORK

Gives substantial recovery over a short period of time.

SHADOW BREW

The melee boost and invisibility this potion provides is perfect for stealthy attacks.

STRENGTH POTION

Steel yourself for a fight and increase your melee damage with this drink.

SWIFTNESS POTION

This brew increases your movement speed for 20 seconds.

TNT

TNT can be thrown at enemies and can help you defeat several mobs in one swift move. Just be sure to get out of the blast radius once you have thrown the TNT.

SQUID COAST

As you embark on your quest to rid the land of evil, you witness the plight of the Villagers first-hand. Squid Coast, once a thriving town, is burning thanks to the evil Arch-Illager and his minions. Follow them through the area – and make haste, for the Villagers are in need of you.

VILLAGERS HAVE FLED THEIR HOME, LEAVING POSSESSIONS BEHIND

"Since it is the first level, we wanted to show what the effects of war are on a peaceful area and show the player what could happen to the world unless they do something."

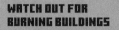

WATCH OUT FOR
BURNING BUILDINGS

VINDICATORS HAVE
LEFT SQUID COAST
IN RUINS

THE VILLAGERS WON'T MIND
YOU USING THEIR PRODUCE
TO AID YOUR QUEST

SKELETONS HAVE ALSO
JOINED THE FRAY

YOUR CAMP

You were too late to save the Villagers at Squid Coast, but all is not lost if you have anything to do with it. Your next step is to set up camp just outside the village – this is where you will return after completing each mission. Take some time to look around, for there is more here than you might expect …

EMERALD CHEST

There are several Emerald chests around the campsite, and more appear as your level increases. Keep exploring to discover them all.

WANDERING TRADER

The Wandering Trader strikes a hard bargain, offering an item appropriate for your level in exchange for an ever-increasing quantity of Emeralds.

BLACKSMITH

The Blacksmith will trade your Emeralds for a randomised piece of gear. The higher your level, the better the gear will be. There's also a Mason who will give you Diamond Dust in exchange for Emeralds. Diamond Dust can be used to increase the Power Level of a piece of gear.

MISSION SELECT

This helpful map shows you which missions you have completed, or are yet to attempt. Click on a mission to see the level of difficulty, drops you may receive and the Artifacts you could be rewarded with.

"We wanted camp to really feel like a safe haven in an otherwise stormy world or something to that effect.

FIENDISH FOES

The Arch-Illager has a villainous arsenal of evils at his disposal, from his loyal Illager minions to the zombies, creepers and skeletons of the Overworld. The subsequent pages will explore each nefarious nemesis in turn, with tips on what to expect when you enter battle, and how to best them once and for all!

THE ILLAGERS

These malicious menaces are members of a cruel society in which the strong rule over all. Until the Arch-Illager came along, they never posed a threat to the peace of the Overworld. Now Illager bands roam freely, causing destruction and woe. Get to know each vile variant below.

PILLAGERS

Armed with crossbows, pillagers are slow-moving but capable of inflicting great damage with a single shot. You will have more luck defeating the pillager by dodging their attacks and getting close for a strong melee attack.

VINDICATOR

These axe-wielding terrors are surprisingly quick on their feet. They'll charge at you in a frenzy and attempt to mow you down with one swift chop. It can be difficult to react quickly with a bow, so try to hit them with a melee weapon before they can hurt you.

ENCHANTER

Recognisable by their strange hats and the magical tomes they clutch in their mottled hands, enchanters can boost the ability of other nearby mobs by creating a magical link to them. The link will be broken if you defeat the enchanter, so take them down first before the other mobs.

GEOMANCER

These magic-wielding Illagers have the ability to manipulate the very ground you stand on. They raise stone pillars and walls out of the terrain to block your path. Beware any pillars that light up, as these will explode after a few seconds. Dispatch geomancers quickly with a bow before they can cause too much strife and trap you.

EVOKER

Experienced adventurers may well have encountered evokers before. They will summon a stream of fangs out of the ground to hurt approaching heroes, then call in a group of vexes to finish you off. Step aside to avoid the worst of the fang attack, and defeat the vex with a melee weapon before finally beating up the evoker.

ROYAL GUARD

Protected by heavy armor and wielding both a shield and spiked club, the Royal Guard are not easily defeated. Your first attack will destroy their shield but cause no damage. Pelt with arrows to keep them at a distance. They're slower than most mobs so you should be able to keep this up to deplete their health.

FAMILIAR FOES

Seasoned adventurers will know this horde of horrors well. They appear throughout the land – often in large groups, which makes them particularly tricky to deal with. Use the following strategies to ensure your victory.

CREEPER

To stop creepers blowing you up, take them out with a bow from a distance or hit them quickly before they go boom!

SPIDER

Spiders shoot webs to snare heroes, which can slow you down, but a quick melee hit is all you need to defeat them.

SKELETON

These emaciated mobs rely on a bow to harm heroes. Reply in kind with your own ranged weapon to eliminate them.

ZOMBIE

Slow and shambling, zombies are easily beaten with melee attacks. Be warned: the armored zombie requires many more hits to take it down.

BABY ZOMBIE

These diminutive devils are much speedier than the full-size variants, but can be brushed aside with one hit.

CHICKEN JOCKEY

This mysterious alliance of chicken and baby zombie is another quick-moving enemy. They're more of an annoyance than a danger, so focus on bigger threats first and foremost.

CHICKEN JOCKEY TOWER

Shoot this odd creature with a bow first. The chicken will fall, causing the baby zombies to scatter. Then cleave through the horde to fully defeat the mob.

HUSK

These brutes are similar to zombies in terms of speed but have better defence. Shoot them with a ranged weapon so you can keep away from their powerful attacks.

FURTHER FOES

You won't see these faces quite as often as those on the previous pages, but you'll need to know them just as well. Make sure you're fully aware of where they might be lurking and study their behaviour to give you the upper hand in battle.

WITCH

Witches are most common in Soggy Swamp, but can sometimes be found elsewhere. They concoct and throw foul brews, so should be attacked from a distance. You ought to steer clear of the noxious potion clouds to avoid any ill effect.

SLIME

Like witches, slimes also prefer the dampness of the swamp. They multiply when damaged, so quick attacks are best to despatch these gelatinous beasts.

CAVE SPIDER

These arachnids are full of poison and like to bite! They're a plague of underground locales like Redstone Mines. Use a bow to attack them and stay out of range of their vicious fangs.

SKELETON HORSEMAN

If you see a white horse, beware: when you approach, it will transform into four skeleton horsemen. These large mobs need constant damage to defeat and are best dealt with using a powerful ranged weapon.

ENDERMAN

Endermen are notorious for teleporting away after taking damage. Whether you choose a melee or ranged approach, make sure to stand close to a wall so they can't apparate behind you. Prepare for a tricky fight!

MOB SPAWNER

These monster factories spew out waves of hostile mobs until they are destroyed. Heroes can easily be swarmed, so try to hit them with a ranged weapon while fending off as many spawned mobs as you can, then finish off the remaining mobs.

NEW ADVERSARIES

Terrible new abominations have appeared in certain corners of the land and allied themselves with the Arch-Illager. These two specimens are particularly vile – they summon unnatural energies and can quickly overpower even the bravest hero.

WRAITH

THE THREAT

From a distance, these airborne Undead horrors will create areas of scorching blue flames on the ground, which cause significant damage over time and constrict the space you have to manoeuvre in during a fight. To make matters worse they'll also teleport away from you and their own path of flames to avoid taking damage.

YOUR STRATEGY

If you see wraiths among a horde of mobs, try to defeat them before you tackle the other enemies. They are best dealt with from a distance with a ranged weapon to give you the greatest chance of avoiding the blue flames.

THE THREAT

Another Undead horror, necromancers use their staffs to summon zombies and skeletons to carry out their dirty work. They will also rapidly fire damaging bolts from their staff to make dealing with their summoned minions even harder!

NECROMANCER

YOUR STRATEGY

The best way to defeat a necromancer is to keep your distance and shoot it with a bow – ideally one enchanted with Multishot so you can hit the summoned mobs at the same time as the necromancer. If you are forced into melee combat, try to hide in a corner to avoid being swarmed by skeletons and zombies.

THE WORLD OF DUNGEONS

You've been armed with knowledge of the world's beasts and the arsenal of weapons at your disposal to smite them, but it would be wise to familiarise yourself with the many wonderful and varied lands that await you beyond Squid Coast. Journey forth with haste, brave adventurer.

USE NARROW BRIDGES
TO STOP MOBS
SURROUNDING YOU

FREE THE INNOCENT
VILLAGERS!

VINDICATORS
PATROL TO DETER
ESCAPE ATTEMPTS

THE EMBERS OF THE
CAMPFIRE OFFER
LITTLE SOLACE

THE DARK FOREST IS
CRAWLING WITH CREEPERS

FUNGI LIGHT THE WOODS
WITH AN EERIE GLOW

THE ILLAGERS HAVE
CONSTRUCTED
RUDIMENTARY JAILS

CREEPER WOODS

Somewhere in the woods, a caravan is transporting Villager prisoners to
labour in far-off lands. Your first quest is to find the caravan in this mob-
infested maze and stop the Illagers, or there's no telling what dreadful
fate will befall our Villager friends.

CREEPER WOODS: OBSERVATIONS

As you forge a path through the shadowy thicket in pursuit of the kidnapped Villagers, keep an eye on your surroundings. You'll be faced with many dangers from all directions, but there are also helpful items that can aid you on your quest.

TRICKY TERRAIN

As if fending off waves of vicious mobs wasn't enough, Creeper Woods is a particularly difficult area to navigate thanks to the dim light and narrow rope bridge walkways.

CREEPER STATUES

As you make your way through the trees you'll see giant creeper heads and totems, which certainly add to the spooky tone of the area.

EQUIPMENT DROPS

Mobs will often drop swords, armor, arrow bundles and potions when defeated. Keep an eye out for these useful valuables.

INVENTORY CHEST

You'll find an Inventory Chest in each new location, which contains an arrow bundle and a bread loaf.

EMERALD CHEST

Keep an eye out for wooden chests, which are full of Emeralds. They're often found at the very edge of the woods.

EMERALD POTS

These breakable pots appear in the darkest corners of the Woods. Hit them to collect the contents.

LOOK OUT FOR TREASURES AROUND THE VILLAGE BUILDING

IN BETTER TIMES, THE WINDMILLS GROUND THE FARMERS' HARVESTS

THIS VILLAGE LOVES ITS HORSES

FREE VILLAGERS ARE A RARE SIGHT IN THIS LAND

PUMPKIN PASTURES

The Illager raids have brought this fertile land to ruin, apart from one lone village which remains unspoiled. You must warn its Villagers of the danger marching towards them.

THE VILLAGERS' ALARM SYSTEM IS ABOUT TO GET A WORKOUT

DON'T LET THEIR LAND GO TO RUIN

PUMPKIN PASTURES: OBSERVATIONS

Your journey begins in the fields, where pumpkins grow among trees and grassy fields. Closer to the village you'll encounter more of the sights and sounds of Villager life. Here are some things to look out for as you rush to save the Pastures from the Illager attack.

MOB HORDES

Hostile mobs congregate in big groups across Pumpkin Pastures, and the large areas of open space means you can easily find yourself swarmed. If you find yourself in trouble, try to attack them from an enclosed space so you can divide and conquer mobs.

VILLAGER SHIP

The Villagers have constructed a ship by the water's edge in Pumpkin Pastures – perhaps they used it to transport large quantities of pumpkins to far-off lands. Here you will find Emeralds, as well as hostile mobs to battle.

VILLAGE BUILDINGS

As you approach the unspoiled village you will see more and more buildings, some of which contain Emerald pots. Be careful – mobs can hide behind walls and surprise you.

THE VILLAGE BELL

The bell lies at the heart of the village. You must ring it to warn the Villagers that danger is coming. Steel yourself before you do so – as soon as the bell sounds, the Arch-Illager will appear and summon a horde of dangerous mobs in order to thwart your progress.

"Up until this point in development, all levels had been fairly dark and closed in. We wanted to do something different, open, brightly lit farmlands that players could explore.

A DENSE FOG
SHROUDS THE SWAMP

THERE ARE PLENTY OF
POTION INGREDIENTS
LYING AROUND

NO ONE KNOWS WHY
WITCHES ARE SO CRUEL

UNSETTLING SKULL
DECORATIONS SIGNIFY THE
DANGER OF THE SWAMP

VILE GREEN WATER

YOU CAN'T LET THE WITCHES PROVIDE THE ILLAGERS WITH EVEN GREATER POWER

SLIMES ARE A COMMON SIGHT IN THE SWAMP

SOGGY SWAMP

A coven of wicked witches live at the heart of this sinister swamp. They conjure up all manner of brews to empower the Arch-Illager and his ever-growing army. If you don't find and defeat those witches, the Illagers will be unstoppable!

SOGGY SWAMP: OBSERVATIONS

The swamp terrain is uneven and waterlogged, which makes navigating the area tricky – dodge-roll as much as you can. As you make your way across the swamp in search of the witch brews, you will be met with all manner of dangerous mobs, from lowly slimes to The Cauldron.

WITCHES

Concoctors of the witch brews that form the objective in Soggy Swamp, witches are seen in great number. Their sheer number in this location combined with their status-inflicting potential makes them a significant pain. Try to take them out before other mobs.

SLIMES

The family of green slimes are in their element in the Soggy Swamp. They won't cause too many problems for you, just make sure to reduce them to the smallest size and leave them be.

WITCH BREWS

These sit simmering in large cauldrons at the heart of the swamp. It is said that these brews help to control the evil Illagers, so that they are better able to do the Arch-Illager's bidding. Fortunately, they are easily destroyed with a sharp hit from a melee weapon.

THE CAULDRON

This is the first boss mob that the Arch-Illager will summon in his attempt to stop you. The Cauldron produces magical purple fire that deals damage to any who touch it and also conjures up a variety of dangerous mobs to join the fray. Most disturbingly, it can consume dead mobs to regenerate its health! Defeat minor mobs before turning a ranged weapon on the Cauldron itself.

CONJURED SLIMES

REDSTONE MINES

There are unsettling rumblings in the mountains of the Overworld. Rumours suggest that the Illagers are building something dreadful far beneath these already-deep ancient mines – something of soot, metal and flame. Only a hero could brave the cavernous underground and uncover the truth.

WHAT COULD THE ILLAGERS BE BUILDING WITH ALL THIS REDSTONE?

ILLAGERS PATROL THE MINES TO MAKE SURE EVERYONE IS WORKING HARD

THE RICHES OF THE MOUNTAIN ARE BEING FERRIED ELSEWHERE

REDSTONE MINES: OBSERVATIONS

The Redstone Mines are a claustrophobic network of narrow tunnels and speedy cartways, with perilous drops at every turn. What follows is an account of some of the things you will be faced with in your quest to free the Villager prisoners.

MINECARTS

Fast-moving minecarts emerge frequently from tunnels. Try to avoid walking on the tracks as much as possible – minecarts will cause significant damage if they hit you.

DEADLY LAVA

Be very careful not to touch the lava, for it will surely spell your doom. Lava runs freely through the mines, due to the Illagers' excavation in search of precious redstone.

CAVE SPIDERS

Lurking in the cobwebbed corners of the mine are droves of these eight-legged menaces. While they can be easily dealt with, they can cause a problem in numbers, so stay agile as you attack.

MOB SPAWNERS

Smart heroes would do well to seek out these devices first and foremost. They may not cause any damage, but you'll end up needing to vanquish fewer mobs!

IMPRISONED VILLAGERS

Before you can escape the mines, you must locate the imprisoned Villagers. They are in the deepest parts of the mines, being forced to dig for redstone.

REDSTONE GOLEM

You'll encounter this unnatural beast – another product of the Arch-Illager – at the end of the mine. It smashes its arms into the ground, creating deadly shockwaves that can damage and disorient you in equal measure.

THE MINED REDSTONE
HAS REACHED ITS
DESTINATION

VINDICATORS
OVERSEE PRODUCTION
OF MYRIAD TERRORS

FIERY FORGE

The Fiery Forge is where the Arch-Illager builds monstrous machines that devastate the villages of the Overworld. He must be stopped at all cost, so strike with everything you've got and raze this forge to ruins. Beware – you will find it heavily guarded.

ONE OF THE FIERY
FORGE'S CREATIONS
IS ALSO ITS DEFENDER

THE ILLAGERS' MACHINES
OF WAR ARE CREATED IN
THIS FACTORY

SEARING HOT LAVA
BUBBLES OMINOUSLY
IN THE FORGE

FIERY FORGE: OBSERVATIONS

The Fiery Forge lies at the very centre of the Illager war machine, a place where mighty weapons are created to destroy all you hold dear. But stopping it will mean facing the mightiest weapon that the Illagers have yet forged ...

REDSTONE CORES

These cores are highly explosive and seem to have something to do with powering the Arch-Illager's unnatural redstone creations. Your mission is to activate them all, so that the Arch-Illager cannot put them to use. Beware a nasty surprise on destroying the last core – make sure you've sharpened your best weapon before you do so!

LIBRARY

What dark secrets are being woven in these halls of dread learning? This is where the enchanters' spell books are being imbued with power to enhance their fellow Illagers in battle. Move swiftly, and beware surprise attacks from between the bookcases.

REDSTONE CUBES

These cubes roll towards heroes, dealing damage on contact. It is rumoured they also – somehow – assist Illagers with their mining endeavours. Cubes can be deftly defeated using melee attacks.

This enormous boss is a variant of the redstone golem. It possesses the same shockwave attack as the golem, and can also summon redstone cubes to attack heroes. Fend off the cubes first then turn your attention to the Monstrosity. Artifacts that increase your defence are useful, as are those that give you a chance to instantly revive – you might need to ...

THE DEAD RISE FROM THE REMNANTS OF A LOST CIVILISATION

WHEN THE DEAD WALK, THEIR MASTER IS NEVER FAR AWAY

HUSKS ARE MORE POWERFUL THAN YOUR REGULAR ZOMBIE

CACTI CANYON

The Arch-Illager seeks to summon armies of the Undead using a power that rests deep within an ancient desert temple. Finding the temple, however, is an adventure in its own right. The entrance lies hidden somewhere in this canyon – a sprawling maze of paths filled with malevolent mobs and lost secrets.

DEEP RAVINES CUT THROUGH THE AREA

PRICKLY CACTI MANAGE TO SURVIVE IN THIS HARSH LANDSCAPE

OUR ADVENTURE TAKES US TO THE BARREN DESERT

CACTI CANYON: OBSERVATIONS

Cacti Canyon is a barren and dusty place, overrun with dangerous enemies. You must keep them at bay as you attempt to navigate the confusing terrain. Let us hope that you are able to stay alive long enough to locate the desert temple.

HIGH GROUND

The land is uneven and broken up by deep ravines. Keep an eye out for skeleton archers, which may shoot at you from higher ground as you make your way through narrow paths between hills.

GUIDING BEACONS

Your first task is to activate beacons that will reveal hidden walkways and lead you to the temple. You will find them to be heavily guarded by the Illagers.

LOCKED GATEWAY

The desert temple is well protected – hidden behind locked gateways that can only be opened with the aid of key golems. Fortunately, the key golems will not be far away. Beware – upon opening the gateway you will be greeted by a horde of skeletons, zombies and Illagers.

KEY TO THE CANYON

Key golems are prevalent in the labyrinth of the Cacti Canyon, hiding in the dark corners away from any raging battles. You'll need to find many of these along the way in order to find the temple entrance – just make sure they don't get hurt and run away!

The canyon level went through several concept stages. What we did know was that we wanted a level with large vistas and deep natural formed canyons.

TOUGH AND IMPLACABLE, THE
SKELETON VANGUARD HAVE
STOOD GUARD FOR CENTURIES

THE BEAUTY OF AN
ANCIENT CIVILISATION
IS NOW CORRUPTED

THE CRAFTSMANSHIP IN
THEIR CONSTRUCTION
IS FABULOUS

DESERT TEMPLE

Deep within these halls awaits a powerful necromancer, the forgotten
ruler of an ancient kingdom. The necromancer wields an enchanted
staff with the power to summon the Undead. You must destroy it
before the Arch-Illager's tiny, evil hands can claim it.

SEEK OUT AND
PROTECT THE
KEY GOLEMS

USE THE RICHES
OF THE PAST TO
AID YOUR JOURNEY

DESERT TEMPLE: OBSERVATIONS

Time has destroyed parts of the temple, yet much of it remains intact deep beneath the surface of the desert. This place is full of old and forbidden magic: necromancy, the darkest sorcery, which the ruler of the Undead has practised since ancient times.

SPRINGING TRAPS

Observant heroes may notice slits spanning the width of some floors. Hidden blades will spin out of them and slice through heroes. There are also crushing walls in some corridors to watch out for.

NECROMANCERS

The Desert Temple is flooded with these practitioners of the evil arts. The unnerving necromancers will summon Undead mobs to attack you, then push you back with beams from their staff. Use a ranged weapon to take them out if you can.

SKELETON VANGUARD

These armored skeletons are The Nameless One's personal guard. Their shields will absorb your first attack, while they slash you with their blade. Persevere with a bow to finish them off without getting too close.

THE NAMELESS ONE

The Nameless One is a boss variant of a necromancer. It summons its skeleton vanguard to attack heroes before joining the fray and targeting you with large, slow-moving projectiles. It can also confuse heroes by creating mirror images of itself.

IN BETTER TIMES, YOU MIGHT EVEN SAY THESE WINDOWS WERE BEAUTIFUL

QUITE THE BRAGGART. AND WHAT'S THAT HE'S POSING WITH?

HIGHBLOCK KEEP

You've made it to the formidable abode of the Arch-Illager. Try not to be distracted by its terrible grandeur, for it crawls with his most trusted soldiers and sorcerers, who are ready to protect their master with their lives.

SYMBOLS OF THE DIMINUTIVE DESPOT'S REIGN OF TERROR HANG FROM THE WALLS

THE ILLAGER ROYAL GUARD ARE LOYAL, STRONG AND NOT ON YOUR SIDE

THE FURNISHINGS SHOW OFF THE ARCH-ILLAGER'S GARISH TASTES

HIGHBLOCK KEEP: OBSERVATIONS

The Arch-Illager certainly knows how to take care of himself –
Highblock Keep is filled with plush rugs, impressive chandeliers and
all manner of delicious food. There seems to be some kind of party
underway, giving heroes an opportunity to spoil the Illagers' fun.

ILLAGER HORDES

You will see every known
variant of Illager here, from
lowly pillagers to the armored
Royal Guard. Focus your
attacks on the deadliest Illagers
first, ideally shooting them
from a safe distance, before
hacking your way through the
hordes. Use Artifacts when you
feel overwhelmed by mobs –
the Corrupted Beacon will be
particularly effective against
such great numbers.

WRAITHS

Wraiths seem to be the only other mob permitted
within the hall. Be on the lookout for blue flames –
run away if you're caught in the inferno – and finish
off the wraiths before dealing with other mobs.

KEY TO ESCAPE

Somewhere in the middle of the dungeon, you
will find a small, open-air courtyard crawling with
zombies and skeletons. Listen out for the key
golem as you battle – you will need it to unlock
the gate that leads back into the halls.

ILLAGER CHEFS

Near the buffet tables, you will see Illagers garbed in chef outfits and brandishing spatulas. They do not appreciate unwanted guests at the banquet. It should only take one or two swift hits with a melee weapon to finish them off. Spatulas do not make for great weapons.

BUFFET TABLES

Destroying one of the several buffet tables will prevent the Illagers from regaining their strength. As an added bonus, you will be rewarded with a cascade of Emeralds each time you destroy one.

THE ARCH-ILLAGER'S THRONE

The Arch-Illager will appear when you reach the throne, summoning several waves of Illagers. Stay on higher ground near the throne and pick off as many Illagers as you can before switching to your melee weapon.

WATCH OUT FOR THE BOLTS FROM THESE FANATICS' CROSSBOWS

OBSIDIAN PINNACLE

The Arch-Illager has fled to the ramparts of the monolithic Obsidian Pinnacle. Make haste and fight your way through to the highest tower. The Arch-Illager's reign of terror ends tonight.

THESE WON'T COME ALIVE, WILL THEY?

ONE OF THE ARCH-ILLAGER'S MOST POWERFUL MINIONS

THE SCENE IS ILLUMINATED BY STORMY SKIES AND FLICKERING FLAMES

NARROW RAMPART

OBSIDIAN PINNACLE: OBSERVATIONS

One more battle and the war will be won! But this battle will be the ultimate test of your skill and bravery, for the Obsidian Pinnacle holds one last terrible secret. Do not proceed until you are equipped with your very best weapons, armor and Artifacts.

SPRING PLATFORMS

These allow you to jump between different areas of the broken rampart. You will likely land right in the middle of a horde of Illagers, so be prepared to fight. If you have a companion with you, you will need to summon it again each time you jump to a new section.

TERROR AT THE TOP

Several redstone golems reside at the top of the Obsidian Pinnacle. Use your best ranged weapon and take care not to fall into lava as you do battle with these creatures.

THE ARCH-ILLAGER

Once you have fought your way through the hordes of Illagers, you will reach the top of the Obsidian Pinnacle and come face to face with the Arch-Illager. What he lacks in height, he makes up for in evil. Since he is not much of a warrior, he will call forth his darkest creation to do his bidding ...

THE HEART OF ENDER

The Heart of Ender has an unnatural power, the likes of which have never been seen. It uses a horrific target attack to strike heroes down, eviscerating them in an instant. You should equip armor that gives you a chance of revival in case it proves too tricky. Perhaps you will be the hero to end The Heart of Ender and the Arch-Illager's evil reign.

ADVANCED QUESTS

If you think you've reached the end of your journey, think again. The adventure is just getting started! Dungeons has many different ways to play, and whole new areas to explore once you've beaten the game. Browse the pages ahead to find out what heroes do once they've saved an entire world.

PLAY STYLES

As your power increases, so does the difficulty of your quest. A wise hero will join forces with up to three other warriors as they revisit each area in search of more valuable loot. The most successful teams are those in which each member chooses a different play style. Here are a few examples for you to try out.

THE TANK

The tank is very difficult to bring down – they wear the strongest armor and smash right into the heart of the fray. Armed with a strong melee weapon, the tank can smash a path through any horde they encounter. They aren't the quickest member of the team, however, since they favour heavy, slightly slower weapons.

LOADOUT

GRAVITY HAMMER	**HEAVY CROSSBOW**	**FULL METAL ARMOR**	**DEATH CAP MUSHROOM**	**CORRUPTED BEACON**	**GOLEM KIT**

THE NINJA

Ninjas are quick on their feet and more than a little bit sneaky. They rely on the element of surprise and attack in swift, subtle movements using only the most lethal weapons. They dart around the edges of a fray, picking off mobs one by one with decisive stabs and rapid arrow fire. They boost their attacks with a variety of Artifacts, favouring those that boost movement speed or stun enemies like Light Feather and Shock Powder.

LOADOUT

DARK KATANA

BUTTERFLY CROSSBOW

SPIDER ARMOR

BOOTS OF SWIFTNESS

SHOCK POWDER

LIGHT FEATHER

THE ARCHER

The archer may not have the strongest armor or melee weapon, but their powerful bow more than makes up for this. They prefer to stay at the edge of the battle, taking out mobs from a distance with glorious sprays of arrow fire. They make use of a number of arrow Artifacts to boost attacks and enjoy alternating between flaming arrows and exploding arrows – watching the archer at work is extemely entertaining in its own right.

LOADOUT

| FANGS OF FROST | HARP CROSSBOW | MERCENARY ARMOR | FIREWORK ARROW | TORMENT QUIVER | FLAMING QUIVER |

THE HEALER

The healer is a gentle soul, in possession of many restorative and protective items. They prefer to stay out of the fight as much as possible, instead spending time healing and buffing allies who are better equipped for battle. This is a very important role that requires much skill, for the healer must remain at their teammates' side, while also maintaining their own health and avoiding combat as much as possible. When forced to do battle, they favour weapons that heal any nearby allies at the same time.

LOADOUT

DIAMOND SWORD

SABREWING

FOX ARMOR

SOUL HEALER

TOTEM OF SHIELDING

TOTEM OF REGENERATION

THE SOUL HUNTER

A terrifying figure to behold, there is something decidedly unnatural about this particular member. The soul hunter lives to gather souls and relies on the mysterious weapons, armor and Artifacts that harvest them, providing unimaginable power. This gives the soul hunter an advantage over most mobs, since their equipment is imbued with the unnatural power of the Undead – perfect for dealing with skeletons, zombies and Illagers alike. Soul-sucking equipment is rare, however.

LOADOUT

| ETERNAL KNIFE | VOIDCALLER | SOUL ROBE | HARVESTER | CORRUPTED BEACON | LIGHTNING ROD |

THE TRICKSTER

Sporting an unassuming Hunter's Armor, many would mistake the trickster for an ordinary townsperson, but that is merely an opening ruse. When the enemy least expects it, the trickster will unleash a volley of arrows from the Imploding Crossbow to draw enemies in. When within reach, they'll face doom at the blade of the legendary Grave Bane polearm. The trickster's Iron Hide Amulet provides a hardy defence that their armor is unable to offer, and their other Artifacts are intended to confuse and constrain enemies.

LOADOUT

GRAVE BANE

IMPLODING CROSSBOW

HUNTER'S ARMOR

IRON HIDE AMULET

WIND HORN

SHOCK POWDER

SIDE DUNGEONS

As you progress through the main dungeons you will notice that several side dungeons appear on your map. These side dungeons provide heroes with an opportunity to hone their combat skills and collect more loot and Emeralds. Here is what awaits you.

CREEPY CRYPT

Located in Creeper Woods, the crypt is not for the faint of heart – the dark corridors are filled with terrifying tombs and crawling with mobs. It is also laden with loot – there are switches that reveal hidden areas and bonus chests that appear as rewards for defeating mob hordes. Your mission is to find the lost tome and make it out in one piece. Beware of crumbling walkways as you explore.

ARCH-HAVEN

Once you've passed through Pumpkin Pastures you can visit Arch-Haven – a coastal settlement at the edge of the pastures. You will begin on a ship and will need to battle your way across the beach, where the Illagers have made themselves quite at home. You must find a series of spellbooks situated on stone plinths throughout. There is also a cave to explore before you head back to the ship and sail away to safety.

SOGGY CAVE

This mysterious cave is full of doorways, each of which leads to a different area of the swamp. You must enter the doorways in the correct order if you want to visit each area, since they are all connected by a confusing series of gateways. In some areas you will need to complete arena battles before you can progress, while others will pose button puzzles to solve before you can lay your hands on valuable prizes.

LOWER TEMPLE

Beneath the main Desert Temple is an area full of skeletons, wraiths and necromancers, as well as the tricky traps that slowed your progress in the upper temple. Keep exploring the maze-like corridors and you will be rewarded with loot for solving puzzles. Once you're finished, you'll need to find a key golem in order to escape.

UNDERHALLS

There's more to Highblock Keep than meets the eye – beneath the regal red rugs is a dusty cellar full of forgotten things. Parts of the cellar look like jails, with chains hanging from the ceiling. Your quest is to fight your way through hordes of mobs, collecting swag as you look for the way out. But you will not be able to pass freely between areas of the cellar – you will need to find a key golem to access the main area, and escaping is no easy task.

SECRET MISSION

At the top left corner of your map, you will see an outcrop of islands labelled '???'. You will find yourself transported to a land filled with giant mushrooms and populated by highly aggressive mooshrooms. How these usually gentle beasts came to be so angry is a mystery, but what is clear is that they can deal serious damage to heroes who enter their territory. Fight your way through the hordes of herds and you will be rewarded with valuable treasure.

THE END?

You've seemingly restored peace to the ravaged Overworld, but your hero's intuition tells you that there are further adventures and greater perils just beyond the horizon. Stay alert, brave warrior, because a hero's work is never truly done ...